Riding
Step by Step

Riding
Step by Step

By Margaret Cabell Self

With photographs by the author

New York: A. S. Barnes and Co., Inc.
London: Thomas Yoseloff Ltd.

© 1965 by A. S. Barnes and Co., Inc.
Library of Congress Catalogue Card Number: 65-13041

A. S. Barnes and Co., Inc.
South Brunswick, New Jersey

Thomas Yoseloff Ltd.
18 Charing Cross Road
London W.C. 2, England

First Printing April, 1965
Second Printing November, 1965
Third Printing July, 1966

6232
Printed in the United States of America

Contents

1 First Steps 9
  Preparing to Mount 10
  Mounting 13
  Adjusting Your Stirrups 17
  How to Sit 21
  Getting the Right Position 27
  Suppling Exercises 29
  The Reins 35
  Dismounting 39
2 The Horse at the Walk 43
  Learning to Communicate with Your Horse 43
  The Aids 44
  The Rein Effects 48
3 The Trot 67
  How the Horse Moves at the Walk and Trot 67
  The Posting Trot 68
  The Sitting Trot 76
4 Some Exercises and Games to Teach Control 79
  The Voltes and Circles at the Trot 79
  The Change of Hands on the Strong Trot 79
  The Half Turn 80
  The Half Turn in Reverse 82
  The Figure 8 83
  The Flank Movements 84
  The Broken Lines 84
  The Pivot Around the Forehand 86
  Pivot on the Hindquarters 89
  Riding in Pairs 91
  Riding in Fours 94
  Some Games to Promote Control 95
  Backing 96
  If Your Horse Rears 99
  If Your Horse Bolts and Tries to Run Away 100

5 Riding Without a Saddle 102
  The Pad and Surcingle 103
  Mounting Without a Saddle 104
  The Position Without a Saddle 104
  Riding at the Walk 106
  Riding at the Trot 107
  Some "Monkey Shines" 108
6 Learning to Canter 119
  How the Horse Moves at the Canter 119
  Learning to Canter in the Saddle 119
  The Leads 120
  Putting the Horse into the Canter 122
  The Difference Between the Canter and the Gallop 126
  Using the Balance Position at the Canter or Gallop 127
  Other Activities 127
7 Handling Your Horse Around the Stable 129
  Entering the Stall 129
  Leading the Horse 134
  Grooming 139
  Bridling the Horse 147
  Saddling the Horse 155
  Taking Off the Saddle and Bridle 161
  Taking Care of Your Tack 166
  Index 171

Riding
Step by Step

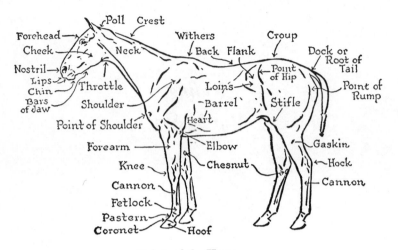

Points of the Horse

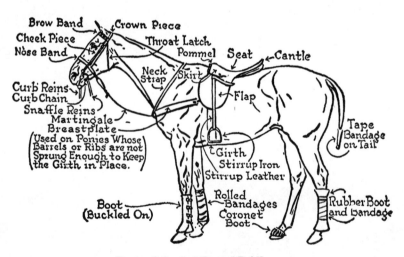

Parts of the Saddle and Bridle

1

First Steps

Almost anyone can get up on a quiet horse and sit there. He may even manage to stay aboard when the horse is moving. But this isn't really riding. Such a rider will not be able to get his horse to do what he wants to do when he wants him to do it. Because the rider doesn't sit properly the horse will be uncomfortable. Because the rider hasn't learned to "talk" to his horse through his legs and hands and the way he uses his body and weight the horse won't understand him. If the horse has any spirit and the rider makes him too unhappy, he may deliberately do something to make the rider unhappy too, such as bucking, rearing or trying to run away. If he is a pluggy, stubborn type of horse he will just stand still and refuse to do anything, knowing that the rider can't control him. In such cases it is the horse who is master, not the rider.

But if the rider will only take the trouble to learn to do things the right way he'll find that he and his horse make a fine team. And he'll find that they can do all sorts of things together that he never dreamed they could do. From the first the rider must realize that when things don't go the way he wants them to it's not the horse's fault. Either the rider has done something wrong or he simply hasn't the experience to know how to do the right thing. This holds true even when a horse is deliberately disobedient and tries to kick another horse or to throw his rider. For if the rider had more experience the horse would never try to get away with such behavior. Knowing that to succeed you have only to become a good rider, that it all depends on you and not on your horse, should be encouraging.

Just reading this book won't make you a good rider, however. You will have to really study the pictures and then practice what you have studied over and over again. But all of it will be fun. First look carefully at the diagrams of the horse, saddle, and bridle and learn the words that are important so that you will understand them when you meet them in the text. Now you are ready to take your first steps as a horseman, so let's begin.

PREPARING TO MOUNT

Go quietly up to your horse opposite his left shoulder. Speak to him first, then check his saddle and bridle to be sure that they are on correctly (see Chapter 7). If stirrups are still run up on the leathers, pull them down. It's a good idea to keep one hand run through your reins and to go around the head of the horse, not behind his tail, while you are checking these things. Be sure that the left stirrup is long enough for you to get your toe in it. If it isn't, let it down a few holes.

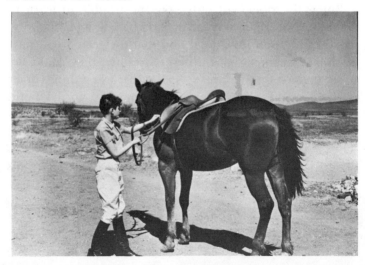

Pick up the buckle of your reins and hold it in your right hand as high as you can.

Grasp the reins just below the buckle with your left hand and slide that hand down to the horse's withers; your forefinger should be between the reins, separating them. Your reins should now be "lightly stretched," tight enough so that you can feel your horse's mouth and can control him but not pulled so taut that he is uncomfortable. Let go the buckle-end of the reins that you are holding in your right hand and let that part of the reins drop onto the right side of the horse's neck. This extra length of rein which is behind the rider's hands when he is holding them is called the "bight."

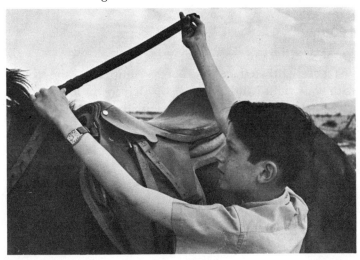

Turn slightly to face your horse's rump. Hold the stirrup with your right hand and put your left toe in it. Grasp the mane a little way up the neck with your left hand, still keeping the reins taut. Put your right hand on the pommel of the saddle.

MOUNTING

Brace your left knee against the saddle, spring from the ball of your right foot, helping yourself by pulling slightly on the mane and pommel with your hands. Stand for an instant in the stirrup, with your left knee straight, and then swing your right knee high over the horse's back. Settle lightly into the saddle and put your right foot into the stirrup.

How not to do it. Don't dig your horse with your toe, as the rider in the photo is doing. Instead, push your toe

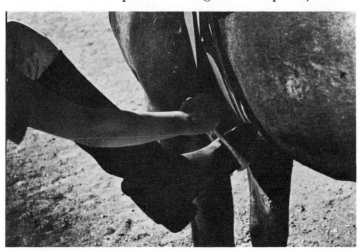

down and, as you turn to face the horse's shoulder, turn it to the front. Don't hit the horse's rump with your right leg as you swing it over his back. Don't drop into the saddle with a "clump." How would you like seventy-five pounds or more dropped onto the middle of your back.

What to do if your horse doesn't stand still for mounting. Some horses try to swing their hind quarters away when you try to mount. If this happens, turn the horse's head slightly away from you by making the right rein a little shorter than the left. Since his head and his hindquarters cannot be in the same place at the same time he will not be able to move his rump to the right. Horsemen have a special phrase to describe this method of controlling the horse's movements. It is called "opposing the hindquarters with the forehand." Perhaps you'll run across this phrase in a book sometime. Later in this book we may use it while describing some equitation exercises.

Some horses try to crowd you by swinging their quarters towards you or even by "cow-kicking" (kicking forwards and to the side with a back leg). To avoid this, stand well forward and make your left rein a little shorter so that the horse's head is now bent towards you. Again you are controlling him by "opposing his hindquarters with his forehand."

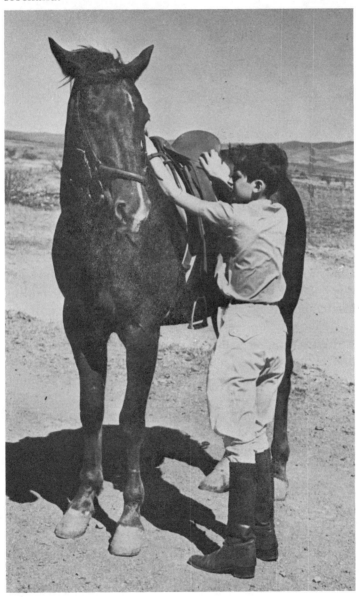

Some horses try to bolt forward when you are mounting. If you think your horse may do this, hold your reins very short, mount very slowly, and the instant you feel him about to move take your left hand off his mane and carry that hand back towards the cantle of the saddle, pulling hard and saying "whoa" or "stand" in a firm voice. If you are part way on, remain standing in your left stirrup, without swinging your right leg over, while you get him under control with your reins. If you drop back to the ground, he'll know he has won. As soon as he is quiet, swing your leg across, catch the other stirrup, then lean forward and pat him. With such a horse it's a good idea to carry a bit of carrot and reward him with a piece as soon as you are in the saddle. He'll soon learn to stand while you are mounting and wait for it.

Some horses try to back away when you are mounting.

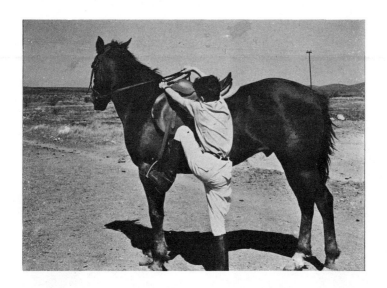

In such a case use the military method of mounting, shown here. The reins are in your right hand, and that hand should be on the pommel of the saddle. Your left hand grasps the mane. Instead of facing the horse's rear you should stand further back, at about the cantle of the saddle, and face front. This method is also an easy way of mounting if your horse is a little tall for you. It is safe to use if you know that your horse won't cow-kick. From this position, you can move backwards with the horse if he tries to back away. If he does back away, give him a sharp slap on the belly, and be sure to wait until he quiets down before you put your toe in the stirrup. Don't forget to reward him with a tidbit after you are mounted.

ADJUSTING YOUR STIRRUPS

Your stirrups must be exactly even and the right length. To measure them, take your feet out of the stirrups and let your legs hang naturally. The tread of the stirrup irons

17

should just hit the middle of the instep. This rider's stirrups are an inch short, though they are a good length for jumping.

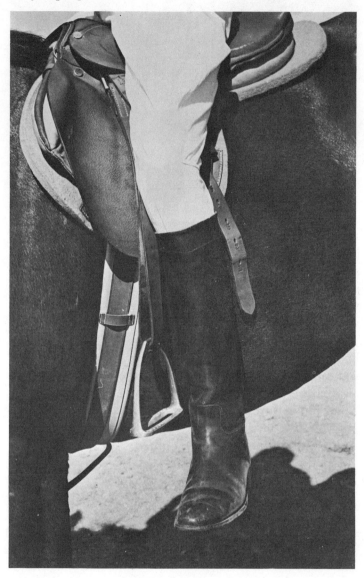

To adjust a stirrup take the reins in one hand; leave your foot in the stirrup but don't put any weight on it. Keep the hand that holds the reins off the horse's withers so that you can control him. With the other hand grasp the end of the stirrup leather near the buckle and pull up. This will open the buckle and pull it away from the iron catch that holds it to the saddle. Now push down on the tread with your foot, letting the strap slide through your fingers until you get the leather the right length. Keep your eyes *up* and make the adjustment by feel.

When you think the length is right, feel for the point of the buckle with your forefinger and, once you have it,

slide it into the nearest hole. Then take your foot out of the stirrup and, by pushing down on the under strap, run the buckle up again where it belongs under the saddle skirt. Now change your reins over and do the other stirrup to match.

In the photo we see the rider's stirrup correctly adjusted. This method of adjusting stirrups, using only one hand and keeping your eyes up, will seem hard at first, but when you have practiced a bit you will be able to adjust your stirrups in only a few seconds even when the horse is moving.

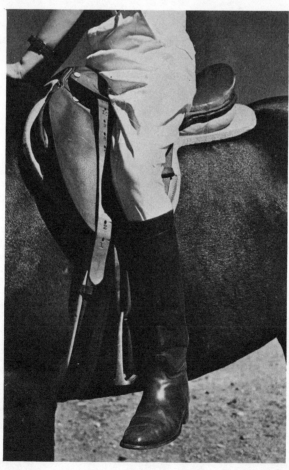

HOW TO SIT

Unless you sit exactly right, you and your horse will both be uncomfortable. Also you will both tire more easily. Notice that this rider is sitting in the deepest part of the saddle which, in a correctly designed saddle, is the exact center. His head is up, his eyes are looking straight ahead. His chest is high, his back is straight. His elbows are slightly bent and slightly ahead of his hips. His hands are neither flat nor stiffly vertical but relaxed and slightly bent. The reins are taut, but not pulling — what the horseman calls "lightly stretched." If you take a ruler and lay it on the picture you will see that a straight line runs from the rider's elbow down his forearm and along the reins to the horse's bit. If you were looking down at the rider from above the line would still appear straight. This means that the rider must carry his hands from six to ten inches apart depending on how thick the horse's neck is. How high above the withers the rider carries his hands will depend on how high the horse holds his head. The hands must always be a few inches in front of the pommel so that when the horse brings his head in the rider can bring his hands back without hitting himself in the tummy.

Notice that the rider is not slumped back on his tail-bone but is sitting upright on his "sitting bones." When you are sitting on your horse put your hand under you and you will feel the points of these two sharp little bones.

Now look at the rider's legs. The angle or slant of the rider's upper leg is about the same angle or slant as the horse's shoulder blade. His lower leg slopes sharply back. His toe is in the stirrup as far as the ball of his foot. The point of the rider's knee and his toe are in a line. If he looks down he cannot see his own toe, for the point of the knee hides it. There is also a vertical line which runs from the rider's ear down through his hip bone to his ankle bone.

In the photo we see the rider from behind. Notice that his ankles are bent slightly inward, with the edge of the outside sole of the boot a little higher than the inside edge. This last is pushed against the inside edge of the stirrup. Since the stirrup is always wider than the rider's foot, you can see in this picture that the extra part of the stirrup must be to the outside and that the tread must lie squarely under the ball, or broadest part, of the foot. Also note that the whole leg is curved snugly against the horse but, because of the foot and ankle position, the rider doesn't have to "grip with his knees" to keep this close contact. It is true that it is the position of the legs of the rider and his balance, not his hands, that keep him on his horse. The idea that he should "squeeze" or "grip hard" at all times to keep from falling is wrong, for two reasons: first, it would be very tiring for the rider, and, second, it would excite the horse and make him unruly.

Notice also that this rider's elbows are close to his sides but that they are hanging naturally and his shoulders are relaxed.

22

How not to do it. Compare the next picture with the other showing the rider from behind. Here the rider's feet are flat, and his knee is so far away from his saddle that you can see the tell-tale triangle of daylight between it and the saddle. This is the sure sign of a beginner, no matter how many years he may have ridden. Although you cannot see his hands you know they are flat, for his elbows are sticking out. When the horse trots or canters the rider will flap his arms like a crow flying home to roost.

In the next photo the rider is sitting too far back in the saddle. His legs are pushed forward and his shoulders back. His elbows are straight. He looks like someone sitting in a rocking chair, not like someone sitting on a horse. If you are sitting in a chair and a leg gives way or someone pulls the chair out from under you, you sit on the floor. But if you sit on a horse correctly and he moves out from under you suddenly this won't happen, for you will be in balance, with your weight over your stirrups instead of on your rump.

In the next photo the rider is slumping, with his tail-bone instead of his sitting bones under him. His reins are too long and his hands high and flat. Thus he couldn't control his horse at all should it try any funny business. Furthermore, his head and eyes are down. If he goes on sitting this way when his horse is in motion, and if the horse stumbles he will very likely do a "forward roll" over the horse's shoulder. And whose fault will that be? Certainly not the horse's!

In the next photo the rider is trying hard to sit correctly but he's much too stiff.

Raise your hands high over your head. Stretch upward — your head too. Pretend someone is hanging you by your ears! Now bring your hands down to your sides, palms out. Keep your chest and upper body elevated but let your shoulders relax. Sit tall.

So much for your upper body. Now let's work on your legs and feet. Rest the tips of your fingers on your horse's withers, with your legs under you but not drawn back, your heels down. Now put your weight on your stirrups and raise your buttocks slightly out of the saddle. Your back must have a hollow in it, it mustn't slump over. Push your buttocks back and bend at the hips. Try to touch the pommel of the saddle with your belt buckle. This is called the "balance position," or "balancing in the stirrups." You'll hear this term many times, so don't forget what it means.

Now put your hands on your waist and see if you can keep this position without pitching too far forward or sitting back in the saddle. If you can, then your thighs,

legs, knees, and feet *must* be in the right position, neither too far forward nor too far back.

How not to do it. The rider in the photo is standing in his stirrups rather than balancing. Don't confuse the two positions.

SUPPLING EXERCISES

Before picking up the reins or moving out, let's try some exercises which will make you limber and agile and give you confidence. Most quiet horses will stand for these. If you are not sure whether yours will or will not, get someone to hold him for you the first time. All good horse-men practice these movements daily not only when the horse is standing but at the different gaits as well.

29

Arm exercises. Reach forward and pat your horse just behind the ears.

Bring your arm in a circle over your head.

Reach back and pat your horse on the rump.

With your left hand reach down and touch your toe without lifting your foot.

With the same hand, reach over and touch your right toe. Now do these exercises with your right hand.

Body exercises. Lean forward and touch your horse's shoulder points with both hands.

Now lie all the way back, cross your arms on your chest, and pretend you are taking a nap. See if you can sit up without moving your hands. Repeat this exercise three or more times.

Cross one leg over in front of you.

Keep on turning on the saddle and cross the other leg over the horse's rump so that you are now sitting in the saddle facing his tail. We call this "going around the world." To get home again you go on around until you are back in position. Then, starting with the other leg over the withers, go around the world the other way. When you become really agile you'll be able to do this exercise with your arms folded.

Leg exercises. Draw one knee up in front of you, balancing on the saddle with your hands on your waist. Let that knee down and draw the other one up, balance, and let it down. Now do both at the same time.

THE REINS

Put the tips of your fingers on your shoulders.

Now bring your hands down in front of you, keeping your elbows and wrists slightly bent, your fingers relaxed.

Look down at your hands and arms. This is how they must look when you are holding your reins.

To get the reins the right length, slide one hand down them to the horse's withers while you hold the bight in the other hand, just as you did in preparing to mount. This is also the correct way to shorten your reins when you are riding if you find them too long.

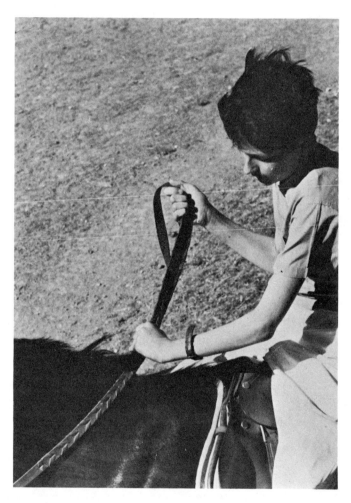

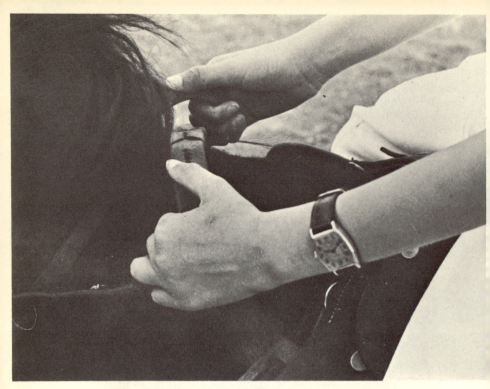

Now take one rein in each hand and hold them as shown, between the ring and little finger. The bight comes out through the thumbs and falls to the right side of the horse's neck. The fingers work on the edges of the reins; the thumb, flat on top, keeps them from slipping.

How not to do it. The rider's hands in the photo are too stiff and are held too close together.

In the next photo the hands are too flat; the rider cannot use his wrists and fingers as he should.

DISMOUNTING

Start by taking your right foot out of the stirrup. Now put your reins into your left hand and put your right hand on the pommel of the saddle. Grasp the horse's mane with your left hand. You are ready now to put your weight on

your left stirrup and swing your right leg over your horse's rump, just as you did in mounting.

Stand for a second on your left stirrup, straighten your knees and elbows and rest your weight on your hands.

With your weight on your hands, take your left foot out
of the stirrup and kick your heels together.

As you drop to the ground, push a little away from the

saddle and turn so that you land facing the same way the horse is. Don't let go of your reins.

2

The Horse at the Walk

LEARNING TO COMMUNICATE WITH YOUR HORSE

You are now ready to start learning horse language. Your horse has been trained to understand and obey certain signals. Now you must learn what these signals are. Also you must understand that when you give a signal and your horse obeys it, you must reward him in some way so that he will understand that he has done what you want. The way you reward him is to stop signalling him.

Let us see how this works. Suppose you want your horse to stop from a walk to a halt. To tell him that this is what you want him to do you sit deep in your saddle and carry your shoulders a little back. At the same time you close your legs lightly on his sides and give gentle little tugs on both reins with your fingers. Your horse will come to a halt because this is how he has been trained. You must then stop these signals. If you don't stop them your horse, thinking you want something different, will start to move backwards. If in your excitement you make your signals stronger he will get very confused and may rear or buck or do something else to show you that he doesn't understand and that you are making him uncomfortable. You are not talking horse language, you are talking a foreign language. So you see how important it is to learn how to communicate with your horse in such a manner that he will both understand and obey you.

As mentioned above, you talk with your horse through your hands on the reins, your legs or heels on his sides, and the way you distribute your weight. These are called the "aids." You may also use your voice (provided it doesn't affect other horses within hearing) and your back.

Of these aids you should use your weight first. The general rule is that you put your weight in the direction in which you want your horse to go. If you want him to go forward you lean a little forward (but without crouching). If you want him to turn to the right you step a little harder on your right stirrup and put more weight on your right "sitting bone." Many sensitive and highly trained horses will obey you when you use your weight alone. But such horses are not suitable for a person who is just learning to ride, for such a rider will always confuse his mount through lack of control of his own body.

The next aids to be used — and these can be used at the same time that you use your weight — are your legs. Your horse has been taught to move his hindquarters away from the pressure of your legs. If you push against his side with your left leg he will move his hindquarters to the right. If you squeeze both legs he will move forward.

Think of your horse as a tricycle. If you are sitting on a tricycle and move the handlebars alone you won't go anywhere. You have to push on the pedals. It is the same with the horse. All movement, whether forward, backward, or to the side, must start with a movement of the hind legs. That's why we said above that your legs must always be used when you want your horse to make any sort of movement, for your legs are what tell the horse to move.

How the hands are used. The hands of the rider must be trained. If the rider uses his hands too strongly, the horse will be made uncomfortable and will not understand what is wanted. Then he will become disobedient. If the hands are not used strongly enough, again the horse will be confused and presently he will refuse to obey at all. The thing that makes developing good and well-educated hands important is that each horse you ride is different. How strongly you use your hands will depend on how the horse reacts. This goes, of course, for the use of the legs as well.

It has often been said that to learn to ride one must first learn to feel what the horse does in response to commands. Then one must learn to understand and interpret what one feels. Finally one learns to influence and control the horse through the aids. There are several different ways of using the hands. Study the pictures carefully after you have read the descriptions, so that you really understand them.

The active hand. We spoke earlier of giving little tugs on the reins using the fingers and wrist. This is called "the use of the active hand." For all basic riding this is the best way to use your hands, for it teaches you to control your horse by "tact" rather than by force.

The rider starts with his hands relaxed. The rein to the horse's mouth must be "lightly stretched." The rider feels a very slight pressure and so does the horse.

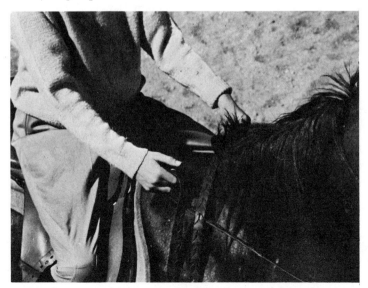

To use the hand actively the rider now closes his fingers on the reins, squeezing them against the edges and perhaps bending the wrists slightly. If the horse is in motion the rider squeezes and releases with each step of the horse. This is called "using the hands in cadence with the horse's stride." The instant the rider feels the horse respond by beginning to slow his gait he stops using his hands actively. In relaxing his hands, however, the rider does not allow the reins to get slack but keeps them lightly stretched so that he can still feel the horse's mouth. Thus he continues "talking" to his horse even when he is standing still.

The passive hand. When we want the horse to do something different from what he is doing we use the active hand. When we want him to go on doing what he has been doing, keeping the same gait and direction, we use what is called the "passive hand." This is difficult, for it means that no matter how the horse carries his head, the rider must move his hands accordingly so that the rein is never too slack or too taut.

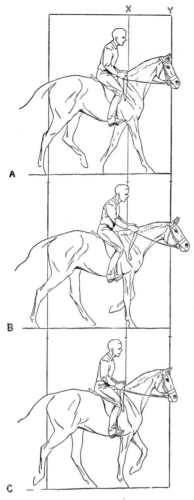

The Passive Hand

Look at the diagram showing the horse walking. Notice that as he walks his head goes up and down, forward and back. At the canter the motion is even stronger. It takes a great deal of practice to learn to follow these movements of the horse's head. Your shoulders, elbows, wrists, and

47

fingers must all be perfectly relaxed. You must let the horse himself pull your hand forward, and then, as he brings his head up and back, you must carry your hand up and back so that you never break the "straight line" which should run from your elbow along the reins to the bit.

It goes without saying that the rider who depends on his hands to keep himself from falling off when his horse moves suddenly or bucks cannot have either an active or a passive hand. Therefore he cannot talk to his horse in proper horse language, and of course cannot control him.

Before going on to the uses of the reins let me explain that there are different types of bridles. Those with a simple jointed mouthpiece taking only one rein are called "snaffle bridles." "Pelhams" and "full bridles," or "Weymouths," have two sets of reins. The lower reins are called "curb" reins and the upper are called "snaffle" reins. The photo shows the rider holding double reins. The snaffle reins are held between the ring and little finger as before. The curb reins are held between the ring and second finger of each hand. You may find double reins a little awkward at first, but you will soon get used to them. Until you do it is best to have the curb rein just a little looser than the snaffle, for the curb is a more severe bit. Think of it as an emergency brake. Ordinarily, you will use only your snaffle reins, and they will probably suffice. If you really need them, however, the curb reins are available to you.

THE REIN EFFECTS

Let us now talk about the different things we can do with our reins, remembering always that in using these "rein effects" we will use an active hand, changing at once

to a passive hand when the horse begins to obey. Also remember that before using the reins at all we must first use our weight and legs.

Here again it is easier to show the rein effects in a

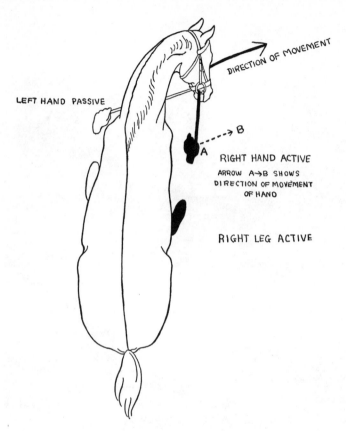

DIRECTION OF MOVEMENT

LEFT HAND PASSIVE

→ B

A

RIGHT HAND ACTIVE

ARROW A→B SHOWS
DIRECTION OF MOVEMENT
OF HAND

RIGHT LEG ACTIVE

The Opening, Leading Rein

diagram than with photographs. There are five rein effects
in all. We'll begin with the first three.

In the diagram showing the *opening, leading* rein. The
rider has carried his right hand a little to the right and is
giving light tugs. The horse has turned his head to the
right and will turn in that direction. The rider will use
both his legs, the right one being held on the girth, the
left being used actively behind the girth. This will cause
the horse to turn in a curve, his hind legs following in the
trace of his front legs. If the rider wanted the horse to turn

50

DIRECTION OF MOVEMENT

B

A

LEFT HAND
PASSIVE

RIGHT HAND ACTIVE
ARROWS A → B SHOWS
DIRECTION OF MOVEMENT
OF HAND

The Indirect Rein

on his center, almost in place, he would use the same rein effect but his right leg would be carried back to push the haunches out as the horse turned.

In the next diagram the rider has carried his right rein slightly to the left so that it presses against the right side of the horse's neck. The horse has turned his head a little to the right, but, because he feels the pressure of the rein on his neck and because the rider's weight is to the left with the right leg pressing against his side just behind the girth, he will move to the left. This is called the *indirect rein effect.*

51

When the rider wishes the horse to slow up or stop he carries both reins straight back. This is called using the reins in *direct opposition*. To oppose something, as you know, is to go against it. In this case the rider is opposing or going against the forward motion of the horse. If the horse is moving fast he will slow his gait. If he is walking he will stop. If he is standing he will move backward. In every case the rider closes his legs on the horse's sides before he uses this rein effect.

Let us now apply what we have learned. You have brought your horse out, mounted, and done the suppling exercises. Before moving out it would be well to check your girth, perhaps pull it up a hole. Many horses tighten their muscles when they are first girthed up. Later they relax and the girth becomes loose. It isn't necessary to dismount in order to tighten your girth. Without taking your left foot out of the stirrup, carry it forward. Put your reins into your right hand and lift the stirrup flap up and hold that with your right hand also. Now take hold of the billet strap as shown, with your fingers on top and your thumb underneath, just as you did when you shortened your stirrup leathers. Pull up on the billet strap, feel for the hole, and slip the tongue of the buckle into it using your thumb and forefinger.

Turning your horse and moving him forward. You are standing in the center of the arena and you want to turn your horse to the right and make him follow along the track near the wall or fence. To do this you need to use all your aids, as follows. Put your weight into your right stirrup and on your right sitting-bone. As you do so, push against the horse's barrel with your left leg and heel a

little behind the girth. At the same time raise your right hand up and to the side, as shown in the picture. This turns the horse's head and breaks up any resistance he may have. Give little squeezes with your hand and pushes with your leg until the horse has turned into a nice, smooth curve and is walking along the track. Then go back to the passive hand and leg. As he walks along push with your back as though you were making a swing go higher, but be sure all your aids are used in cadence with his stride.

Turning a corner. From the very beginning learn to turn a corner correctly and make sure you don't get careless and sloppy. Most horses will try and cut across the corner, as you see in the photo, instead of bending their body out into it and staying close to the wall.

It does no good to try to steer your horse into the corner by using the hand to the wall in a leading rein effect, as the rider in the next photo has done. All the horse does is turn his head into the corner; his body is still way away from the wall.

The next photo shows the correct way to make a horse go out into a corner. Look closely and you will see that the rider is using his inside (left in this case) indirect rein with his left leg a little behind the girth but almost on it. As shown in the diagram on page 51, the horse is turning his head to the left, which is the direction in which he is traveling, but he is actually moving his body to the right, toward the corner as he makes the turn. The rider's leg is like a pivot around which the horse curves his body.

Riding a small circle or "volte" (VOLtay). A very good way for you to learn to control your horse is to practice coming away from the wall every now and then and riding a small circle about twenty feet in diameter. Start at a given point on the wall, close both legs on your horse, and

put your weight onto the inside (left, in the photo) stirrup. Now carry your left hand a little to the left and upward, using a leading rein effect and bending your horse's head slightly to the left. When he feels you use your aids he will turn off the track. Your problem now is to make him make a nice, round circle, not too big and not too small.

Balancing your aids in demanding the circle. Think of the horse's spine, from poll to dock, as bending in a curve as his feet describe the circle. This means that his head must not be pulled too far in to the center and that his hind feet must follow exactly in the track of his forefeet. You will have to feel exactly what he is doing. If the circle starts to get too small, use your inside leg against his side at the girth and carry your left rein against his neck as you did in turning the corner so that he increases the size of the circle. If he starts to swing his hind legs off the track and the circle becomes more like a series of straight lines than a curve, then you should carry your outside leg behind the girth and give strong pushes against his quarters, at the same time using your left hand very actively on the leading rein.

Try and complete the circle just where you started it. Continue along the track and then make another circle. Make four or more until you are back to where you started, then change direction as described below and make an equal number of circles going the other way.

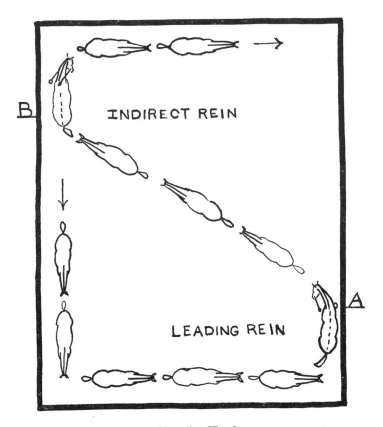

Changing Hands

Changing direction. A very good way to change direction is the one shown in the diagram. It is called "changing hands" or "changing reins." As you see in the diagram, the rider continues on the track until he turns a corner from a short wall onto one of the long walls of the arena. He then follows the track for one stride (about ten feet), turns away from it, and rides on a diagonal line straight across the arena to a point about ten feet from the end of the opposite long wall. Here he turns and follows the track.

He is now riding in the opposite direction. In making these turns make the horse bend properly, as you did on the circles, balancing your aids according to how he reacts. Then ride on a straight line until you come to the opposite wall. After you have turned onto the track be sure and make him bend out into the corner, using an inside indirect rein, an inside leg on the girth, and your weight on the outside stirrup.

Learning to halt correctly. The second exercise for control is to stop your horse properly. Many poor horsemen try to stop just by leaning back and pulling, like the rider in the photo. The horse will probably stop in time but his hind feet will be too far behind and his nose will be pushed forward and out.

Some riders try to stop by raising their hands and leaning forward. If you do this, generally the horse won't stop at all, for in leaning forward you are telling the horse to keep on going.

The rider in the next photo stopped correctly. He first sat deep in the saddle and carried his shoulders very slightly back. Then he closed his legs on his horse (so that the horse would bring his own legs in under him) and began using his hands actively, carrying the reins straight back (direct rein of opposition). The horse has come to a halt with his head drawn a little in, his legs squarely under him. The rider will now relax his aids but will still keep the rein lightly stretched.

More about halting. Sometimes, in halting, the horse will turn off the track with his front feet, as shown in the photo. In this case the rider should use the hand toward the wall a little more strongly than the other.

Some horses stop with their hind legs off the track. To correct this carry the inside leg back a little and use the inside hand a little more actively.

Vaulting off the moving horse. Here is a final and very important exercise. It will make you agile and help take away any fear you may have of falling. Put the horse on the track at the walk. Take both feet out of your stirrups and let them dangle. Now ask a friend to blow a whistle or shout "off." As soon as you hear the signal, grasp the mane of your horse with your left hand (your reins should be in this hand, as when you dismounted in the ordinary way) and the pommel of your saddle with your right hand, lean forward on your tummy, and swing your right leg high over his rump. As you slide to the ground try to push away

from the saddle, turn to the front, and land on the balls of both feet with your knees bent. Don't let go of the reins. You will find that your horse stops of his own accord. Practice this exercise at least five times each time you ride. Later you will learn to do it at the trot and canter.

3

The Trot

When the horse walks his feet are lifted and returned to the track one at a time, one–two–three–four, one–two–three–four. You can feel him moving under you but his back remains level and you are not bounced around much.

At the trot the horse moves differently. He lifts and plants his diagonal legs together. Thus, first he moves his right front and left hind, then, just before they touch the ground, he lifts his left front and right hind. At the fast trot there is an instant when all four feet are off the ground.

This gait feels very different from the walk. Until you have learned to follow the movement of the horse under you you will find yourself bouncing up and down on the saddle just like a golf ball on a hard surface.

There are two things you can do to prevent this, and you must learn to do both. One is to sit deep in the saddle and with each step of the horse give a little push down with your back, letting your tummy push forward and your buttocks push under you. The other is to rise or "post" to the trot. Inasmuch as this last is easier, we'll discuss it first.

THE POSTING TROT

Since the horse moves his legs two at a time instead of singly, the cadence of the trot is one–two — one–two. Start by practicing standing on the ground with your hands on your waist. Now jump your feet apart and bend your knees as shown in the picture. You are now in the correct position

68

to sit in the saddle. Just imagine that someone has ridden a horse up under you. Next watch while someone rides a horse around the arena and listen to the cadence. Straighten your knees slightly and bend them again in time to the horse's trot and count aloud, "up–down — up–down." Isn't that easy?

Practicing on a standing horse. The next step is to get on the horse and take the balance position as you learned in Chapter 1. Be sure your head is up, eyes straight ahead, back straight but sloping forward, not vertical, and that your buttocks are only a couple of inches off the seat of the saddle. This is the "up" position of posting to the trot. Again ask someone to trot a horse around the arena and try to go up and down in time with him, counting aloud as you do so. If you have trouble getting into the "up" or balance position and staying there it is because, as you come down, your legs are swinging forward. If you feel as though you were going to topple forward you are probably dropping your eyes, hunching your back, and letting your

legs and heels go up and back. At first you may help yourself to balance by resting the tips of your fingers on the horse's withers. But within a very few minutes you should be able to do this exercise with your hands on your waist while the horse is standing still. Don't go on to the next step until you can.

Practicing with the horse at the walk. Now you are going to do the same exercise, but with your horse at the walk. If your horse has been trained to keep out to the wall while following another horse and you have a leader you won't have any trouble, but if you are by yourself you may have to ask a friend to run along beside you at first to keep your horse going steadily. When the horse is walking smoothly take a balance position and hold it for three or four steps. Now drop back into the saddle and go right up again and hold the balance position for several steps. Repeat this exercise several times until it becomes easy. Next see if you can go up and then down again with each step of the horse.

Remember that you must not straighten your knees and
stand up high, as shown here. Rather the motion is forward
and back, your buttocks only a few inches off the saddle,
your hips well bent, your back hollowed.

Learning to post at the trot. You are now ready to try
posting while the horse is trotting. First take a light grip
on the mane or neck strap and balance in your stirrups.
Now, with your legs, possibly helped by your voice, get
your horse trotting. Stay balanced a moment, then come
down and go right up again. Listen to the count of the
beating of his feet and say "up–down, up–down" with the
cadence.

At first you may find yourself staying down too long and
getting a couple of rough bounces. Or you may stay up too
long and come back into the saddle just as the horse's body

71

is coming up. This too is uncomfortable. To cure either of these, start over with the balance position and hold on to the mane. Listen to the cadence, say it aloud a few times, and then start going up and down with it. Most young people can learn to post in time to the rhythm in less than ten minutes.

Posting with one hand on your waist. As soon as you feel secure, put your reins in the hand toward the wall, let go the neck strap, and put the other hand on your waist. Be sure not to pull the hand holding the reins up in order to keep your balance. If you do your horse will stop. If the horse tries to cut in from the wall, make the wall rein a little shorter than the other. You can even take the tip of the reins in one hand and put both hands on your waist; then you'll know you aren't pulling on your horse's mouth to support yourself.

Posting with the hands in normal position. As soon as you can post readily without pulling on your horse's mouth and without bouncing, it is time to try posting while holding the reins in the normal way. But here you will find that you run into some difficulty. We spoke, in the last chapter, of the passive hand and how it must follow the movements of the horse's head and always keep the rein "lightly stretched." In Chapter 1 we noticed that there should always be a straight line running from the rider's elbow down the rein to the horse's bit. When the horse trots he does not move his head much, but when the rider posts, his own body goes up and down. The tendency is for his hands to go up along with his body, as you see in the photo, thus breaking that straight line which we want to maintain. If your reins are not too long, but lightly stretched, you will be giving your horse a little jab in the mouth each time you rise to the trot. He won't like this and he won't trot evenly.

An exercise to prevent your hands from bobbing. To avoid this you will have to straighten your elbows slightly each time you rise in the stirrups, bending them again as you come down. The way to practice this is to extend your little fingers and, with one rein in each hand, held short enough so they don't sag in loops, touch the ends of your little finger on each side of the withers just in front of the pommel of the saddle, as the rider in the photo is doing. Now see if you can trot and post all the way around the ring once without letting your little fingers bounce off his neck. It isn't as easy as it looks, but with a little practice you'll find yourself pushing your hands down as you rise without even thinking about it.

The diagonals. As we have learned, the horse moves his diagonal legs in pairs alternately as he trots. Many riders get in the habit of always rising on the same diagonal. Every time the horse's left front leg and right back leg come forward, for example, the rider rises; when the other pair come forward he sits. This is not good for the horse. Since there is more weight on his back when the rider is down in the saddle than there is when the rider is up, one set of muscles will become stronger than the other. Also, if the rider goes out for several hours and trots most of the time without changing his diagonal, he will tire the horse more than necessary.

As your horse walks, glance down at his shoulder blades and you will see that first one and then the other moves forward. Practice rising when the shoulder blade that is next to the wall goes forward, sitting when it comes back. Now put the horse into the trot and post, watching the shoulder blades as before. If you are going to the left, you should rise as the *right* leg moves forward (see page 70). This is called posting on the *right diagonal,* the correct one in this case. Below, the rider is posting on the *left diagonal;* he is up in the saddle as his horse plants his *left* front foot. When you are riding in the arena change your diagonal by bouncing one step or balancing one step each

time you change direction and get in the habit of always posting on the outside diagonal. On the trail change diagonals at least once every ten minutes.

THE SITTING TROT

Let's talk about learning to sit to the trot. This is easier if you start by taking your feet out of your stirrups. Without slumping your shoulders or hunching your back, let all your weight sink down onto your sitting bones. Your hands should be low over the saddle, ready to rest lightly on the pommel to steady yourself. Your shoulders can be a little back to start with. Above all, the lower part of your back must be perfectly relaxed.

Using your back. Put the horse at a walk and pretend that you are going to push the saddle forward and out from under you by sliding it forward using your buttocks and sitting bones. Give a shove, letting your tummy come forward and your tail-bone go under you, relax, and, at the next step of the horse, shove again. The motion is exactly the same as the one you use when pumping to make a swing go higher.

Go around the arena several times practicing this motion. Rest, then go again in the other direction. If your horse tends to walk a little faster with longer strides you will know you are using your back correctly.

When you are sure you have the right motion, you can try it for just a few steps at the very slow jog trot. It is best to have someone lead the horse for you at this point and only go five or six steps at a time. At first you will find that you bounce badly and slide from side to side. Your tendency will be to grip the sides of your horse with your legs. If you do, two things will happen: you will bounce harder and your horse will try to trot faster, for that is what you are telling him to do.

Walk again for a few steps, then try it again. Listen to the sound of the horse's steps and push with your back in cadence, push–rest, push–rest, push–rest.

Even though you find it hard, don't give up but practice the sitting trot without stirrups for five or ten minutes every time you ride.

The sitting trot with stirrups. You will find this even harder than the sitting trot without stirrups, because if you put even the least little pressure on your stirrups and tighten your legs at all you will bounce badly. A good way to learn to do it is to put one hand under you as you trot and then try to push down on your hand with each step

of the horse. If you do this right you will feel your sitting bones digging into your hand.

Keep practicing every day, both with and without stirrups, until you can trot at a regular speed around and around with no separation between your buttocks and the seat of the saddle.

4

Some Exercises and Games to Teach Control

Now that you have learned both the sitting and posting trot you should go back to the exercises given in Chapter 2, which you practiced at the walk. These were the small circles, or voltes, and the change of hands. These you must now practice at the trot.

THE VOLTES AND CIRCLES AT THE TROT

Starting with the voltes, take up the posting trot, and start along the long wall of the arena. As you reach the center-point change to the sitting trot and, using your back with each step of the horse to keep him moving out, ride a volte. On returning to the wall start posting again until you reach the center point of the next wall, which will be a short wall. Again sit the trot while you execute your volte, and so forth.

THE CHANGE OF HANDS ON THE STRONG TROT

When you are once more at your starting point and have turned the corner and taken one stride, take your horse across the ring on a change of hands. Post while doing this, and each time you rise in the stirrups squeeze hard with your legs and at the same time put more tension on your reins. Try and get the horse to drop his head and lean a little on the bit. You want him to take long strides,

and to do this he has to get his weight forward. Sometimes by dropping your hands quite low on each side of the withers and keeping a steady, rather tight rein you will help him to understand what you want, but you must use very strong legs or he will slow down. This is called the *strong trot*. It is not the same as the *fast* trot in which the cadence is more rapid as the horse steps quickly but with short steps.

As you reach the diagonal corner, sit the trot, get your horse to shorten his strides by using an active hand, turn the corner, and start posting until you reach the center point of the wall. Then start the voltes again as described.

THE HALF TURN

In addition to the voltes there is a very good exercise for you to practice called the *half turn*. Notice that the path which the horse follows is shaped somewhat like half an ice-cream cone with a big scoop of ice cream on top. To execute it ride to the center of the long wall, then, at the sitting trot, make a half circle, the same size as the voltes

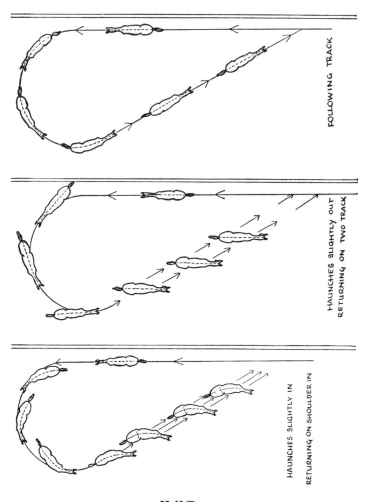

FOLLOWING TRACK

HAUNCHES SLIGHTLY OUT
RETURNING ON TWO TRACK

HAUNCHES SLIGHTLY IN
RETURNING ON SHOULDER IN

Half Turns

that you have been doing. But instead of completing the circle and continuing on the track in the same direction in which you were traveling before, ride diagonally back to the track and you will find yourself going in the opposite direction.

There is another form of the half turn called the *half turn in reverse*. The shape of the figure is the same, but this time you ride away from the wall on a slant until you are about twenty feet from it, then make a half circle back to it and continue on the track.

In doing these don't forget to use all your aids and to balance them so that the horse doesn't make the turn too sharply and so that he maintains an even gait, not suddenly

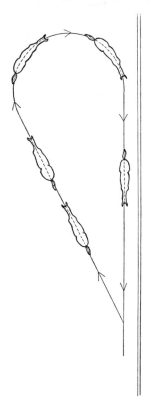

The Half Turn in Reverse

moving out and then slowing down. Sit the trot until the figure is completed, using your back to keep the horse moving smoothly.

THE FIGURE 8

The diagram shows the proper execution of a figure 8. This should not be hard for you now, for you have been practicing the voltes both at the walk and trot. Start from the halt, facing the center point of one of the short walls and about twenty feet from it. Make a round circle to the right, come straight toward the center point as you finish and execute a similar circle to the left. Of course all these figures are at the sitting trot, for you need to use your back to keep your horse moving properly.

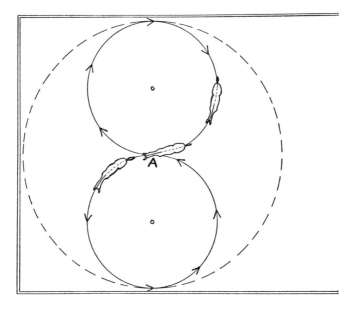

The Figure 8

To make a *flank movement* the rider at the walk or trot turns off the track at a right angle, rides straight across the ring, and turns again. In a turn of this kind the rider should use a strong leading rein and a strong *inside* leg behind the girth. If you are turning to the right you will use your right rein and right leg. This will cause your horse to turn on his center, swinging his hindquarters off the track.

THE BROKEN LINES

Another pattern is called *broken lines*. It is harder than the flank movements, for the horse is asked to swing like a gate, making a small circle about three feet in diameter with his hind legs and a big one about ten feet in diameter

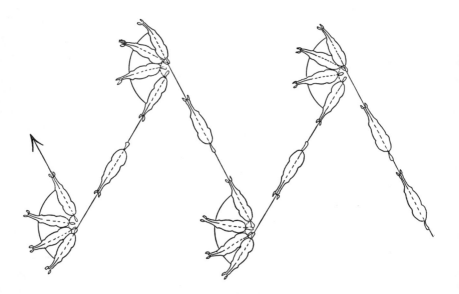

Broken Lines

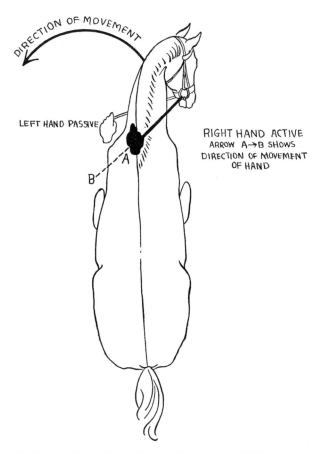

DIRECTION OF MOVEMENT

LEFT HAND PASSIVE

RIGHT HAND ACTIVE
ARROW A→B SHOWS
DIRECTION OF MOVEMENT
OF HAND

A

B

Indirect Rein of Opposition in Front of the Withers

with his front legs. The aids to be used are a little different
from those you used before, for they employ the fourth
rein effect, called the *indirect rein of opposition in front
of the withers.* This is just like the indirect rein which you
used before, in that you bring your rein against the horse's
neck, but instead of just carrying it to the side you also
pull a little back, the direction of the pull being towards

your own hip. If you are using your right rein, the pull will be back and toward your own left hip. This will cause the horse to put his weight back on his own left haunch. At the same time you must carry your outside (right) leg back and push him sideways with it. Your weight must be well back and down in the saddle and over your left sitting bone. You will know when the horse is moving correctly, for you will feel him swing under you. As soon as he has completed the turn, move him forward on the broken lines pattern as shown in the diagram. Don't try this at the trot until you can do it smoothly at the walk.

THE PIVOT AROUND THE FOREHAND

Now you must learn to get more exact control of your horse's hindquarters. The photo shows a rider doing the movement. Your goal is to cause the horse to keep one front leg in position, lifting it and putting it down again as nearly on the same spot as possible while he turns in a half circle, stepping sideways with his hind feet.

Here's how you do it, but remember that you must balance your aids one against the other, correcting when the horse moves too fast or too far. At first he should step just one step at a time, stopping after each step; then, much later, you can ask him to complete the movement without stopping completely.

Stop your horse on the track about three feet from the wall with the center of the ring to your left and the wall to your right. Sit deep in the saddle and gather your reins a little to show your horse that he is to be asked to do something. When you feel that he is alert and ready, carry your right heel back about six inches behind the girth.

Now give a squeeze with your right hand, carrying it
straight back slightly, turning the horse's head until you
can see the bulge of his eye. At the same time push with
your right leg. Keep pushing with your leg until he steps
with his hind legs, carrying his quarters to the left. Don't

relax your left rein or your horse will turn to the right with his forehand. If you feel that he is about to do so, squeeze harder with your left rein and, at the same time, carry your right rein against his neck, changing it from a right leading rein to a right indirect rein of opposition. Keep your eyes up!

The instant you feel the horse step with his hind legs, relax your legs completely, relax your hands so that you have just a light feel on the horse's mouth and praise him. Then repeat the application of your aids so that he takes one more step.

It takes six steps to turn a complete half circle, and the last two are the hardest. Don't be surprised if your horse doesn't pivot perfectly at first. Keep trying and don't lose patience. Later when he can do the half pivot in both

directions you can teach him the full pivot. To do this you will have to stand in the center of the ring, but the aids are the same.

PIVOT ON THE HINDQUARTERS

You did this while the horse was moving in the figure called broken lines. Now you are going to ask your horse to swing his forehand around his hindquarters, while staying in place. He should move one step at a time,

keeping one hind foot more or less in place. Use the same aids as described for the broken lines, but keep your weight well down in the saddle and keep using your back to prevent the horse from backing up.

All the above exercises can be practiced while you are riding alone. If you have a companion, you can ride in pairs at the walk and trot. This is not as easy as it looks, for every time you turn a corner the inside horse tends to get a little ahead. Also most horses don't like to go exactly abreast. For this reason riding in pairs and later in fours is an excellent exercise to teach control.

There is a right and a wrong way to get into pairs. If you are moving around the ring to the left (the inside of the ring on your left and the wall on your right) this is how you do it. Start with both riders on the track one behind the other at the walk. The first rider will be number one, the second number two. Now, while the first rider continues to walk the second rider takes up a slow trot and comes up to the left of the first rider, coming down again to a walk as soon as he is abreast of him. The knees of the riders should be six inches apart and the toes three inches.

As you approach the corner of the ring the outside rider begins to use his legs and back to keep his horse walking fast. The inside rider now uses a left indirect rein of opposition, carrying his left rein against the horse's neck and pulling towards his own right hip; at the same time he puts his weight on his right stirrups and pushes against the girth with his left leg. This has the effect of slowing the horse down slightly and, at the same time, pushing out into the corner and towards his companion.

Riding in pairs at the trot. It is sometimes easier to keep the horses abreast at the trot than at the walk, for there is more variety of speed. In any event, the goal and the aids used are the same.

Getting into pairs when riding on the right hand. To form pairs when moving with the inside of the arena on your right the procedure is a little different. Since to avoid confusion the number two rider must always come up on the left of the number one, number one will have to move off the track to the right so that number two can ride forward along the rail until he is beside him. Remember that the second rider always increases his gait to come up beside the first rider.

Forming pairs at the trot. There is another way to form pairs which is perhaps easier than the one described. In this both riders are on the track at the trot, one behind the other. When a signal or command is given to form pairs, the number one rider comes at once to a walk and the number two rider continues at the trot until he is abreast of the number one rider. They may then both continue at the trot or continue at the walk.

Going back to riding single file from pairs. To resume their original positions; number two rider behind number one, number one keeps on at the same gait, while number two decreases the gait (from a trot to a walk or from a walk to a halt) and falls in behind number two.

Now that you know how to ride in pairs just going straight around you can practice all the figures you have learned — the voltes, the figure eights, and the half turns — and see if you can do them without letting one horse get ahead of or behind the other. The only figure that will be different will be the flank movement. Here, since both horses will turn with the same movement, they will cross the ring one behind the other, forming a pair again when they make the turn on the opposite wall.

RIDING IN FOURS

Riding in fours is much more difficult than riding in pairs, but the principle is the same. If the riders are on

the track in single file, the leading rider, number one, maintains his gait and the others increase theirs until they are beside the leading rider. In turning the corners the inside horse has to slow way down to keep from going ahead, and the outside horse must quicken up a bit but without changing gait.

For more elaborate formations suitable for eight or more riders, see the mounted drill section in the book *Fun on Horseback*, by this author; also "Musical Rides" and "Square Dancing on Horseback" in the same book.

SOME GAMES TO PROMOTE CONTROL

You will need at least four riders for these games; from six to ten riders are better.

Musical Stalls. This is one of the most popular games. Bars are laid on the ground. You will need the same number of bars as there are riders, which will give you one too few stalls. Now you need someone to blow a whistle. The game starts with everyone riding around the arena on the track at a trot. When the whistle blows, all ride to one wall (previously decided on), and turn into the stalls from that side, stopping when they are within the stalls. If a horse steps across a bar or moves forward out of the stall he has to go around again. If two horses come into a stall at the same moment, both have to go out and around again. Since there is always one fewer stalls than riders, one rider will be left out. He or she leaves the ring, a bar is removed, and the game goes on until only one rider is left.

Musical Sacks. This is based on the same principle as Musical Stalls, but instead of bars, feed sacks are laid in a circle with one fewer sacks than there are players. When the whistle blows, all riders come off the track and race for a sack. On reaching it they jump off their horses and put one foot on the sack. They may not ride through the center if they miss the sack the first time, but must lead around the outside to another sack.

BACKING

Your horse has been trained to move backwards readily, but to get him to do this correctly you must use the proper aids. Gather your reins so that you feel his mouth. Next close your legs on him so that he knows you want him to move. Now give strong squeezes on the reins, using them directly in opposition but releasing them with each step of the horse. You don't want him to run backwards; you want him to take one step at a time. His head should be slightly drawn in but only far enough so that his nose is vertical, never in to his chest. He should move smoothly and freely and halt the instant you stop using your aids.

How not to do it. The rider in the next photo is trying to make her horse back up just by pulling on the reins steadily and without using her legs. It's the same horse, but look how awkwardly he is moving, with his mouth open and his nose extended, showing how uncomfortable he is!

Once in a while we run across a horse that tends to stand on his hind legs when the rider asks him to do something he doesn't want to do. There is nothing dangerous in this provided the rider doesn't panic and pull hard on the horse's mouth. And it's an easy vice to cure. As he goes up, throw your weight forward, and the instant he comes down draw your right rein under your right stirrup, as shown here. Pull the horse's nose right down to your toe and kick hard with the other leg. This will be very uncomfortable for the horse; he will find himself forced to turn sharply in little circles; he can't possibly rear. Usually one such lesson is enough to cure him, but if he tries it again use the same method, only harder.

Many beginning riders are terrified of the idea of going fast. Actually it's no harder to stay aboard a horse that is galloping flat out than one that is just cantering. But there is one sure way of stopping a runaway and that is by the use of the "pulley rein effect," as shown here. The rider shortens his reins and gets his weight back. Then he drops his left hand and grasps the horse's mane, holding tightly to the rein at the same time. He raises his right hand up and pulls back and to the side as hard as he can. This will have the effect of turning the horse very sharply. Notice in this picture that the horse has his haunches way under him, and the rider, preparing for the turn, is looking to her right.

Red Light. This is a very good game for beginners, as it can be played at either a walk or a trot. One person is "it." He takes his place in the center of one short wall of the arena and faces the wall. The other players now line up at the opposite end of the arena. The person who is "it" now counts slowly from one to ten and then says "Red Light." While he is counting, those on the other wall may move forward, but they must stop before he finishes. When, on saying "Red Light," he turns around, anyone moving has to go back to the beginning and start over. The first person to reach the one who is "it" has to tag him (not his horse). Then all the players ride back to the starting line, while the one who was "it" tries to tag one of them on the way back.

5

Riding Without a Saddle

Before you can hope to develop hands and legs sensitive enough to allow you to talk intelligently to your horse you must develop a completely secure seat. You will realize why this is true if you think for a moment. If you need to use your hands *or* your legs to keep from falling off when the horse moves suddenly, then you cannot at the same time use them to direct and control him.

The expert horseman keeps his position in the saddle by constantly adjusting his balance. He does not pull on the reins or grip with his legs unless he does so to direct his horse. Consequently the horse learns to react immediately when he feels the rider applying any of the aids. And if a beginner then gets on him and tries to keep his balance through gripping or pulling, small wonder that the horse becomes confused and soon stops obeying altogether!

What is the best way to acquire such a secure seat? Authorities disagree, but in my opinion riding without a saddle and practicing without the use of reins is the only short cut. Obviously, if you have no stirrups you cannot depend on these. If you ride with your hands on your waist you cannot depend on your reins. There remains only one habit which you must avoid from the beginning. You must not grip with your knees but must ride with your legs completely relaxed.

It is perfectly possible to learn to ride without a saddle on a bareback horse. If, however, you can get a pad or an old blanket and a piece of equipment called a *surcingle* you will find these much less slippery than the naturally silky coat of the horse. The ordinary surcingle is just a wide web strap with a buckle and leather tongue.

Putting on the pad and surcingle. If you use a blanket it should be doubled then doubled again and probably doubled once more until it is small enough in area. Place it ahead of the withers and slide it back into place. In putting on the surcingle, throw the buckle end over the horse's back and reach under his belly for it. If you throw the strap end over you will find it much more difficult to tighten and the end will not lie flat. Buckle it snugly in the same position that you would place the girth of the saddle.

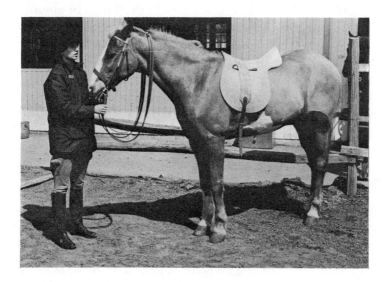

MOUNTING WITHOUT A SADDLE

Unless you are very active you will need help in mounting at first. Stand facing your horse's shoulder and take up your reins as you normally would. Now have your assistant hold your ankle as shown in the picture. She should bend her knees and you should bend your own left knee slightly. You and your assistant should now count in unison, "one, two, three — up." On the word "up" your assistant lifts, at the same time straightening her knees, while you spring. Carry your right leg as high as you do in mounting the normal way and try to land gently on your horse's back in order not to startle him.

THE POSITION WITHOUT A SADDLE

Before taking up your reins, reach high over your head to straighten your upper body. Then pick up your reins and hold them as usual, a few inches apart and a few inches

in front of the withers. Be sure your fingers, wrists, elbows, and shoulders are all completely relaxed. Let your legs hang naturally under you, don't draw them up or push them out stiffly. Your heels will now be higher than your toes, since you have no stirrups; this is not important at this stage. The photo shows a rider sitting correctly.

In the next photo the rider is hunched over and her legs are drawn back with her heels digging into the horse's sides.

Now you must practice all the exercises, the voltes, changes of hands, figure 8's, flank movements, broken lines, etc., at the walk. You will notice that you can feel much more readily what your horse is doing under you. Be conscious of this and keep yourself close to him as he moves, pushing with your back as described in Chapter 3. You must also practice the suppling exercises, swinging first one arm and then the other in big circles as you move around the ring. Twist your head and shoulders as you swing your arm back to touch the horse's rump; let your eyes follow your hand as it reaches over your head and down to your toe. If your horse will walk quietly around the ring and keep out to the wall on his own, or if there is another rider whom he can follow, you can tie your reins in a knot to shorten them and let them hang on his neck just in front of the withers. If you are riding alone and he keeps cutting in to the center, hold the buckle of the reins in the hand that is toward the wall and put this hand on your waist while you exercise one hand. Then do a half turn or a change of hands to change direction, and put your reins in the other hand to exercise the first.

Don't neglect your legs. Pretend you are holding a pencil

with your toes and draw imaginary circles, first with one foot and then the other. Swing your legs forward and back but without touching the horse's sides. Draw up one knee and then the other. All these movements will teach you to adjust your balance and to be independent of your legs in maintaining your seat.

RIDING AT THE TROT

There is one more very important factor. If you take a beach ball and blow it up until it is hard it will bounce much higher than if you put only a little air in it so that it remains soft. If you keep yourself completely relaxed so that your buttocks remain soft you will not tend to bounce nearly as much as you will if you harden them by tightening your muscles.

In taking up the trot it is permissible at first to let your shoulders come very slightly back. This will keep you from hunching over, which is what most people try to do at first. Later try and sit exactly as you do at the walk. Be sure to keep your hands low. If you like you may put a stirrup leather around your horse's neck and, until you learn to adjust your balance, hook one forefinger over this, as shown here.

Start by trotting once around the ring. Then walk for a moment and try again. As soon as you feel secure, try trotting a few steps with your hands on your waist. When you can go two or three times around the arena with your hands on your waist and with your legs relaxed, begin practicing the suppling exercises with your arms, head, and legs. Next work on the schooling movements, the voltes, half-turns, etc. You can easily tell when you are relaxed and sitting correctly, for your horse will go quietly, without trying to cut in, go too fast, or go too slowly. Another way to tell is to sit on the palm of your hand, as you did in learning the sitting trot in the saddle, and feel if you are keeping your weight on your sitting-bones without bouncing.

SOME "MONKEY SHINES"

In Chapter 1 of this book you learned "going around the world" and other good exercises. You will find these much easier to do on a pad than you did in the saddle. Here are some more difficult "monkey shines" which you can begin to practice.

The Scissors. This looks very tricky, and so it is. You'll have to practice it slowly at first, but once you get the knack you'll find it easy.

The rider starts by putting both hands on his horse's withers and leaning his weight on them, as shown here.

Next he brings his legs high up behind him and crosses them in mid-air.

He turns his body also, and as he comes down on the horse pushes himself upright with his hands, ending by sitting on his horse facing the rump.

He now returns to his original position by repeating the movement, resting his hands on the horse's rump, swinging his legs high and crossing them over the horse's withers.

To learn the scissors lie face down on your horse's back, turn your head to the left, bring your right leg under your left, and push yourself up into position. You can also

practice this exercise on your bed until you learn to fling your legs high and cross them in the air, twisting your body as you do so.

Vaulting on from the side. You will need rather a small horse or a pony while you are learning this. If you haven't such an animal, perhaps you can make a little wooden ramp to help you. It need only be two feet wide, three feet long, and should be about six inches high at the higher end. In placing it, put it opposite the horse's shoulder and about eight inches away from him.

To vault on a standing horse from the side, take three or four running steps; when you reach the pony put one hand on his back and one on his neck, then bounce up off the balls of your feet, straightening your arms as you do so. Some riders find it easier to put their elbows on the pony instead of their hands, as shown in the photo.

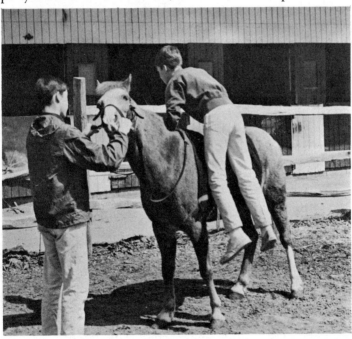

When you are high enough, swing your right leg over and land sitting on the horse. To complete the movement, vault off the horse's right side. Later you can learn to vault completely over a small horse or pony, but you will have to be sure to hang on to his neck until you have landed safely on your feet.

Vaulting on over the rump. Again you will need a small animal that is quiet and will stand for "monkey shines." Run up from behind, put both hands on his rump, and spring upward, spreading your legs apart. Try to land on the top of his rump, or, if you are very active, leapfrog

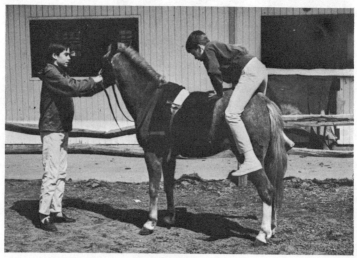

forward on your hands and land in the saddle position. Don't land on the tender loins if you can help it. If you close your knees together a little as you land you'll come down more gently.

And if you're very active you may be able to vault on over the rump and land standing, as the rider in the photo has done.

Standing up on the horse. To stand up on a quiet horse is not at all hard. Start by putting your hands on your horse's withers, resting your weight on them, and then draw your legs up under you, as shown in the photo. Notice

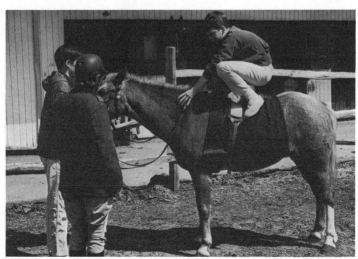

in all the pictures that an assistant holds the pony still by taking one rein in each hand and holding the reins about elbow high.

You'll feel a little insecure and very high up at first, but you'll soon think nothing of standing on your horse.

Jumping Around. The rider in the photo is jumping around. It's really much easier than it looks. He'll end up standing facing the tail, then he'll jump back again.

Perhaps you'll need a little help the first time. Get a friend to hold your right hand with his right hand, as

shown in the photo. This will steady you as you turn and land.

Jumping off over the rump. This is very easy, just step onto the rump and spring off. Land on the balls of your feet with your knees slightly bent.

When you can do everything described in this chapter, you will be well on the way to becoming a good horseman. Furthermore, you will find that, in addition to having attained a secure and independent seat at the walk and trot, you have lost any fear of falling that you may have had before.

How the Horse Moves at the Canter

6

Learning to Canter

We come now to the canter, which is quite different from the trot. You may find it hard at first, and perhaps a little frightening, but once you have learned to sit correctly, letting your body follow the movements of your horse, you will enjoy cantering more than trotting.

HOW THE HORSE MOVES AT THE CANTER

Let us see just what the horse does when he canters. We learned that at the walk each foot touched the ground separately from the others, the horse's back remained more or less level, with little motion, and the cadence of the gait was one—two—three—four. At the trot the horse moved his legs diagonally, the cadence was one—two, one—two, with a period of suspension in which the horse's body dropped rather suddenly out from under us.

In the canter the horse springs from one foot and brings the other three down in rapid sequence, with one back and one front touching almost simultaneously, and we have a cadence of three beats.

LEARNING TO CANTER IN THE SADDLE

When you first try the slow canter in the saddle you may find yourself bouncing badly. It is best to practice this on the longe if you can so that you won't have to

worry about having to control your horse at the same time. The pushing of the back without putting weight on your stirrups is what will correct this tendency to bounce. If, in spite of everything, you still find yourself pounding up and down, try making your stirrups slightly longer than usual. Be especially careful to keep your hands down, and use a neck strap. Remember that if your horse starts to go faster it's because you are either squeezing with your legs or are making him uncomfortable by bouncing on his tender loins. If there is a hill near you and your horse is quiet, you will find that cantering uphill is decidedly easier than cantering on the flat.

THE LEADS

Look again at the diagram showing how the horse moves at the canter. Notice that in the second row of figures the horse is shown planting his right hind and right front feet well ahead of the left. This horse is on what we call the *right* lead. When he goes around corners to the right his

inside back leg will be well under him and will act as a
base of support. For this reason the rider is careful, when
riding on a circle or in an arena, to see that his horse is
leading with his inside legs. The photo shows a horse
traveling to the left on the left lead.

The correctly trained horse has been taught to take up the canter from the walk, or even from the halt, without any intervening trotting steps. But the rider cannot hope to get him to do this until he himself has learned to keep his balance at the canter without depending on his reins or the gripping of his knees to maintain his seat.

The gallop depart on the lateral aids. There are two ways to induce the horse to take up the canter from the walk or halt on the correct lead. One is known as the "gallop depart on the lateral aids" and the other as "the gallop depart on the diagonal aids." The young horse and the rider who is just beginning his career as a horseman usually find the gallop depart on the lateral aids the simplest at first, so we'll start with that.

In the photo we see a rider positioning her horse for a gallop depart on the left lead. Using a right leading rein she has turned her horse's head slightly to the right; this frees the horse's left shoulder. She has also, by using her right leg, pushed the horse's haunches off the track to the left; the horse is walking slightly sideways. Next the rider will lift slightly with the reins, push her back, and apply the right leg even more strongly. The horse will go into the canter with his forehand going *up*. The instant he does so, the rider will straighten him out on the track. The gait will be somewhat slower than the ordinary trot and very evenly cadenced. To keep the cadence even and slow, the rider will squeeze and relax her fingers with each stride and push with her back.

As a beginner you will not be able to get a smooth gallop depart at first; you may have to click your voice, or even reach back with a stick and give your horse a little tap behind the flanks. This will not be your horse's fault, it's

just that you haven't learned to "balance your aids" yet. Just keep trying and if your horse breaks into a trot the first few times, speak to him quietly, pull him in gently but firmly, and try again. Above all, once he is cantering, don't forget to straighten him out. He mustn't go around the track like a crab, you know!

The gallop depart on the diagonal aids. It is because of this tendency of the horse to travel crabwise due to having his head turned away from the direction in which he is moving that the more expert rider puts his horse into the gallop or canter on the diagonal aids. In this method the rider keeps the horse straight on the track, using an inside (right, in photo) indirect rein on the neck and an outside (left) leg just behind the girth. The horse shown in the photo is just going into the right lead.

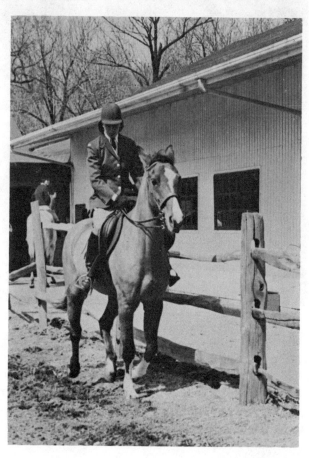

The cross canter. Sometimes an awkward or badly trained horse will "cross canter," that is, he'll lead with one front leg and with the opposite hind leg (right front, left hind, for example). This will feel very bumpy and you should stop your horse immediately and start him over, as he is likely to fall.

The counter canter. In very advanced training of the horse, he is taught to take the "counter canter," leading with the legs next the fence. This is to improve his balance and to make him muscular. The photo shows a horse doing a beautiful counter canter in an arena.

How not to do it. In all the pictures shown you have seen riders who are experienced. Notice how relaxed they are and how calm the horses are. But in the next photo you see a rider who has not had quite so much experience.

Instead of putting the horse into the canter correctly he has used his aids too roughly, consequently his horse has "taken off" with him, showing by his pinned-back ears that he is anything but calm and comfortable. The rider has been thrown out of the saddle and is trying to maintain his balance by gripping with his legs, his heels right up in the horse's sides. This is making the horse go even faster. Furthermore the rider's eyes are down and his back is hunched. If the horse should swerve or stop suddenly, guess who'd find himself sitting on the ground?

THE DIFFERENCE BETWEEN THE CANTER AND THE GALLOP

The canter is a slow form of the gallop. The horse's legs move the same way in both. Indeed, in many parts of the world the term "canter" is not used at all. Instead a slow, a collected, an ordinary, and a strong *gallop* are the four terms used to describe the different rates of speed and length of extension of the stride.

USING THE BALANCE POSITION AT THE CANTER OR GALLOP

Earlier in this chapter we learned that in cantering the rider should sit deep in the saddle and maintain contact with it. At the faster phase, that is, the strong gallop, which is used in racing and in going fast across country, the rider may take up the balance position. This is the same position that has been described before. The rider puts his weight on his stirrups and raises very slightly out of the saddle. If you will look carefully again at the photo showing the horse on the left lead you will see that this rider is using a balance position in the saddle. This position takes much of the weight off the horse's back, enabling him to go faster. It is also very easy for the rider, though he may find it a little tiring at first.

You may wonder why, if it is easier for both horse and rider, one doesn't use the balance position for everything instead of just for racing, hunting, and fast games. The reason is that for more exact control you need to feel and influence your horse by using your back, so continue to sit down in the saddle for ordinary ring work and for competition in equitation classes.

One word of warning. When you first take up the balance position you may find that your horse wants to go faster. Don't be worried; maintain the position but keep a light feel on the reins and use your hands actively to slow him down.

OTHER ACTIVITIES

Now that you have learned all three gaits and are comfortable in them, now that you have learned "horse talk" and can really control your horse and get him to do just what you want, you may want to go on with your riding education. The purpose of this book is just to teach basic control and the right way to handle and sit on your horse. Another book of mine, *Fun on Horseback,* has many suggestions for games, formation riding, hunting, and other activities which you will find useful.

7

Handling Your Horse Around the Stable

From the point of view of safety it is as important to know how to work around your horse when you are on foot as when you are mounted. The horse that is frightened may kick. The horse that is not alert may step on you.

If you don't know the right way to put the equipment on your horse he may take advantage of you and you will spend twenty minutes doing what should take twenty seconds. So let's learn how to do these things correctly.

ENTERING THE STALL

Many horses sleep standing up and with their eyes open. If they are awakened too suddenly they may jump forward in fright or even let fly with their heels. So the first thing to do when you approach your horse's stall is to let him know you're there.

If he is in a box stall, call his name or snap your fingers and get him to turn and face you. Then pat him on the nose, if that's what he likes, to show that you are pleased with him.

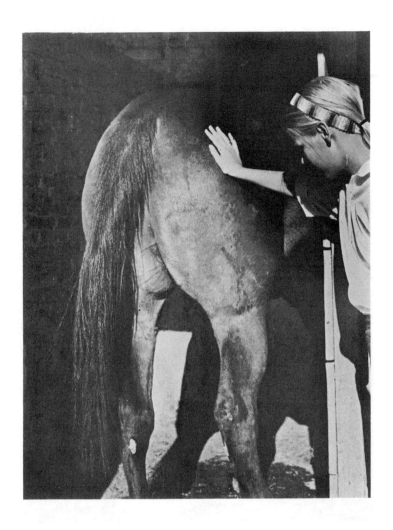

If he's in a standing stall speak to him as you approach
it. Then put your hand gently on his rump and push him
over to the right. Now enter quietly but quickly and go
up to his head.

To back a horse out of a standing stall take the halter
shank (or bridle reins if he is wearing a bridle) in your

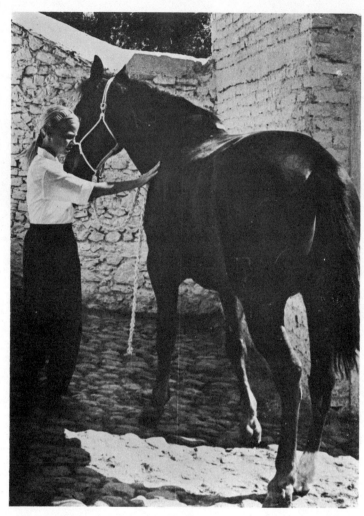

left hand. Put your right hand on his shoulder point. Push
back with both hands and say "back—back!" As he moves
backward, turn his head in the direction in which you
want him to turn. The horse in the picture is being asked
to turn so that he will walk to the left after he is out of his
stall.

To get him out of a box stall, just walk with him, holding the reins and keeping to one side as he steps out.

LEADING THE HORSE

To lead the horse, take the shank a few inches beneath the jaw in your right hand and hold the other end in your left hand. If he is bridled, pull the reins over his ·head and hold them the same way, taking hold of all the reins and slipping the forefinger of your right hand between them, holding the buckle end in your left hand.

Walk out of step with your horse and a little to the side, as this rider is doing, then you won't get stepped on. No horse will step on you on purpose, but if you put your foot in his way he may not notice it.

If the horse already has his saddle and bridle on and you are only going to lead him a few steps, lead him as shown in the photo. Notice that the reins are hanging on the withers and are not over the seat of the saddle.

How not to do it. In the next photo we see an ignorant rider who is trying to lead her horse with the reins across the seat of the saddle and tucked under the stirrup leathers. All she is doing is pulling on the saddle and the horse feels nothing. No wonder he isn't going anywhere!

The next photo shows a careless rider. The ends of the reins are dragging. If the horse doesn't trip over them she probably will. At the worst this could mean a broken bridle, and at the best she will have to ride with muddy, dirty reins!

More about leading. Sometimes it is necessary to lead a horse through a narrow doorway or over a dangerous piece of ground where there are bad holes, sharp rocks, wire, or glass. In such a case you must see that the horse steps carefully or he will hurt himself.

The picture shows you the best way to control him. Take one rein in each hand about ten inches from the bit and keep them level with the horse's mouth. Don't let

the reins get slack as you walk backwards, guiding the horse and not allowing him to step too fast.

Sometimes a horse doesn't want to go with you. Perhaps he thinks he'd rather stay in the stable today. It is no good just trying to pull him straight forward. He will only plant his feet and pull back. Since he is about ten times as heavy

and strong as you are he'll surely win. Instead you must trick him by turning him sharply first to the right . . . and then to the left. He will have to take a step to the side to keep his balance. Once started he'll probably keep going. If he stops again, turn him from one side to the other again.

Cross-tie your horse so that he can't move around too much. Start with the curry comb. This is made of rubber or plastic and has little teeth. Stand on the left and, with a stiff left arm, brush in big circles.

In your right hand carry the body brush, a soft brush with hair bristles. As the dandruff is brought to the surface with the curry comb, sweep it off with light strokes of the brush. Brush in the direction of the growth of the hair, not against it, and finish each stroke by turning and lifting the brush.

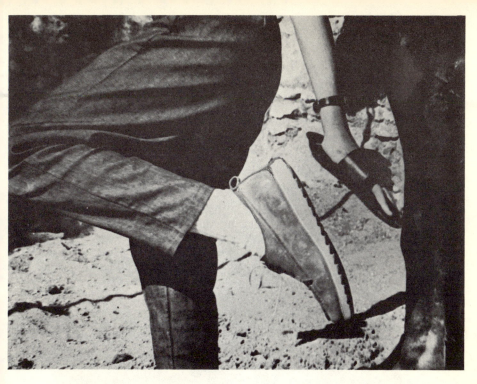

Every few strokes clean the curry comb by tapping it against your heel.

The brush should be cleaned often. This is done by running it over the curry comb.

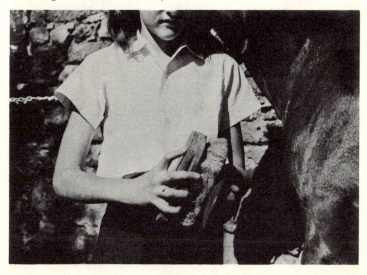

Work all over the body and under the belly. Don't use the curry comb on the lower legs or on the face; you can use the brush on these parts. When you have finished the left side go around and do the right side. You will now have your curry comb in your right hand and your brush in your left.

Next take your hoof pick. Stand, as shown, at the horse's left shoulder facing rear. Lean your weight against his shoulder, slide your hand down his lower leg from the knee to the hoof, and pick up the foot.

Cup his foot in your hand and thoroughly clean the frog and sole. Work from the heel toward the toe so that if the pick slips it will not prick the soft heel.

Put his foot down gently when you have finished. Move to his left back foot, still facing rear. Pick this one up the same way, leaning your weight against his flank to throw his weight onto his opposite leg.

The feet of the horse are the most important things he has. If they are not kept clean they may develop a condition known as "thrush." By cleaning them every day before you ride you can be sure that they are sound and healthy and that there is nothing caught in them.

Comb your horse's mane next and then do his tail. If the tail is tangled, hold it out, as shown, and start at the tips of the hairs and do one wisp at a time. Don't stand directly behind the horse when you do this, but a little to the side. Don't worry about hurting the horse when you do his mane and tail; a horse has no nerves at these points and you can even pull his hair out by the roots and he won't mind. This is often done when the mane and tail are too thick and coarse.

Take up the body cloth and wipe the head thoroughly, especially around the eyes and behind the ears. Now wipe the whole body. If there is any mud on the lower legs,

first rub it off with your fingers and then use the cloth. Be especially careful to clean behind the fetlocks above the heels.

The last thing you do is to run your bare hand over every inch of your horse. As you do so feel for any unusual heat, rough places, cuts, scratches, or bumps. When you have finished your horse should look shining and you will have the satisfaction of knowing that there are no bruises or cuts which you might not have noticed otherwise.

Hold the bridle as shown and stand by the horse's left shoulder, facing front.

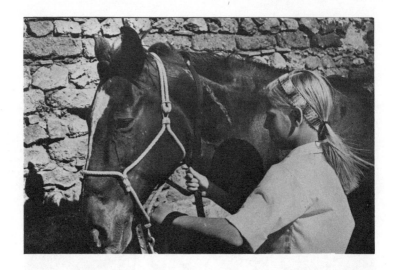

Put the reins over his head and leave them just behind the ears. Thus, if he tries to back away you can grasp them, as shown, and keep control of him. If you put the reins back on the withers he can easily break away from you.

Now, holding the bridle in your right hand by the middle of the head stall, put it up over the horse's head. The bit should rest against the horse's teeth.

Cup the horse's chin in your left hand. Balance the bit on your thumb. As the horse opens his mouth, pull up quickly with your *right* hand, guiding the bit with your left. Don't try and push the bit into his mouth with your left hand; this will take the tension off the cheek straps, and the bit will only fall out of his mouth again when you take your hand away. It is the right hand that gets the bit into the mouth by pulling up on the head stall.

If the horse doesn't open his mouth of his own accord, slip the fingers of your left hand into the right side of his mouth at the bars. He has no teeth there and cannot bite you. You will find that as soon as you touch his bars or

his tongue he will wrinkle his lips and open his mouth. Be quick with your right hand and pull the bit upward into place before he closes his mouth again.

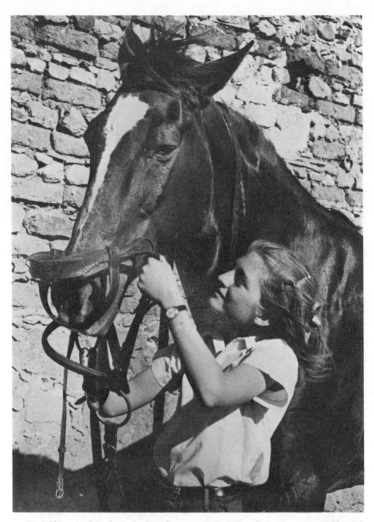

Bridling the head-shy horse or one that is too tall. If your horse is too tall for you to reach his poll, or if he is head-shy or stubborn and holds his head high, his nose pointing to the sky, use the following method.

Hold the bridle as shown by the cheek straps instead of by the crownpiece and stand close under his jaws.

Bring the bridle into position with the bit against the teeth and hold both cheek straps in your right hand, at the same time taking a firm grip on the horse's nose and pulling down if he tries to get away from you. Cup the horse's chin as described above and get his mouth open, keeping the bit in position.

When he opens his mouth pull up on the cheek straps and quickly slip the crownpiece over his ears.

As soon as the bridle is in place, buckle the throat latch. Be sure it is loose enough so you can slide three fingers under it; you don't want to choke your horse.

If your horse is wearing a full bridle or a pelham, un-twist the curb-chain until it lies flat.

Fasten it so that you can get two fingers under it without

disturbing the bit. However, when the reins are drawn slightly back the edge of the chain should come against the jaw.

Finally check all the little "keepers" to be sure they are pushed snugly up and that there are no loose ends of straps which might bother your horse.

If your horse wears a saddle pad to protect the saddle, shake it out well and be sure that it is clean with no dried sweat on the underside. Approach the horse from the left, put the pad on well in front of the withers, and slide it back into place. This makes the hair lie flat under it.

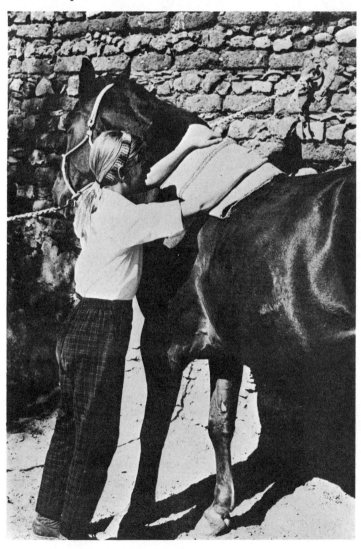

The saddle should have the stirrups run up and the girth should be across the seat. Put it on from the left side. Put your hand on the pommel and shake it to be sure it is firmly in place. The pad should stick out in front of the saddle and should be pushed up into the throat so that it doesn't touch the withers. If your horse wears no pad, or if he wears a shaped pad that is held onto the saddle and goes on with it, put the whole thing on the withers and slide it back. Just be sure that whatever he wears is clean and that nothing touches the high point of the withers.

Go around to the off (right) side of your horse. Take the girth off the saddle. Hold the flap up out of your way with your head and buckle the girth to the billet straps. If there are three of these and your girth has only two buckles use the two outside ones, letting the center strap hang loose on top of the girth.

Now go back to the left side of your horse and reach under him and catch the hanging girth. Bring it up and buckle it as you did on the opposite side. Be sure that the

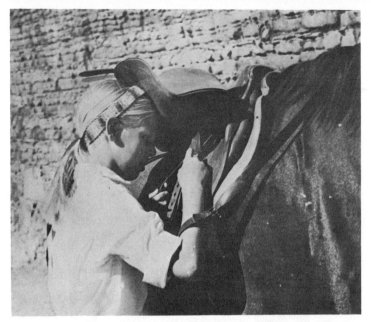

girth is not "lop-sided." If it is fastened on the fourth hole of the billets on one side it should be on the fourth on the other, too.

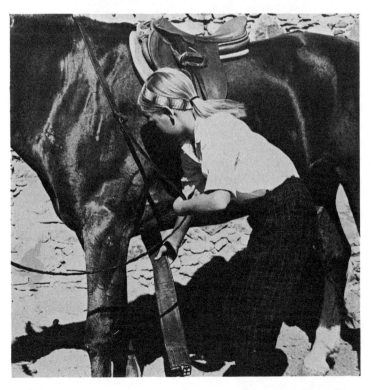

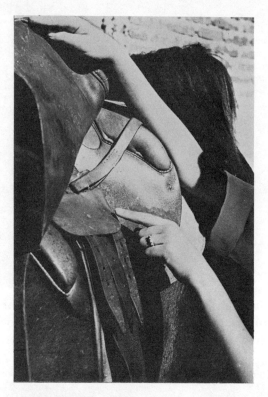

Many saddles have little pieces of slotted leather through which the billets are run above the girth buckles. These are called "girth guards." Their purpose is to cover the buckles of the girth so they don't damage the under part of the flap of the saddle. After you have fastened the girth buckles pull the girth guards down, as shown here. Another thing that is shown clearly in this picture is that the raw edge of the girth should be to the rear and the front or folded edge should be toward the horse's head. This picture is taken from the right side, so the raw, sharp edge is to the left. If, when you pick up your girth to put it on, the raw edge is to the front just turn the whole girth upside down.

Don't make the girth too tight. Fasten it loosely to start with, for the horse's back is cold and he must be used to the feel of the saddle before the girth is tightened. When you do tighten it, adjust it so that you can slip your hand in under it at the bottom of the sweat flaps. Then run your hand down to the bottom of the horse's belly. The girth should feel comfortably snug. It should not pinch. Do this on both sides to ensure that you are not squeezing the wind out of your horse by cinching him up too tight, and also to make the hair lie flat.

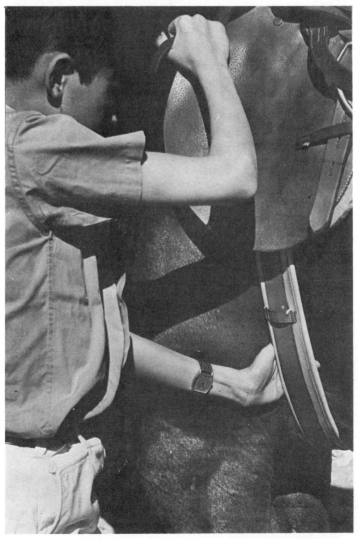

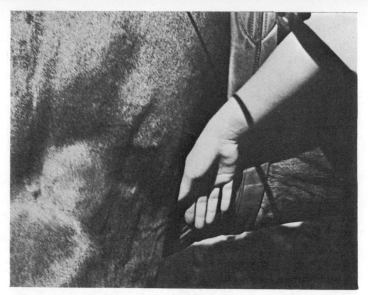

If the saddle is in the correct position there will be a space of about four inches (the width of a person's hand) between the front, folded edge of the girth and the horse's elbow.

How not to do it. The poor horse in the photo has been tacked up all wrong. His brow band is crooked, so is the nose band of his cavesson. His reins are left dangling down on one side. His saddle is much too far back and the pad is not pushed up into the throat. I think he knows something is wrong and is looking around for his rider to come and straighten things out!

If your horse is to stand tied for some time outside his stall, leave the stirrups run up on the irons and tuck the reins under them, as shown in the photo; then he can't get his head down, pull the reins over it, and perhaps step on them. If he could, it would almost always result in a broken check strap.

TAKING OFF THE SADDLE AND BRIDLE

Slide the stirrup irons up on the under stirrup strap and tuck the ends of the straps through the iron (but not through the slot in the tread).

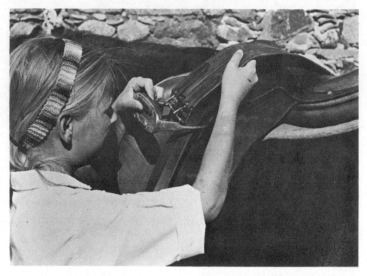

Take off the girth, lay it across the seat, and tuck it into the irons over the stirrup leathers.

Undo the throat latch and curb-chain (if the horse is wearing one), grasp the crownpiece of the bridle together with the reins in your right hand, and slide the whole bridle off.

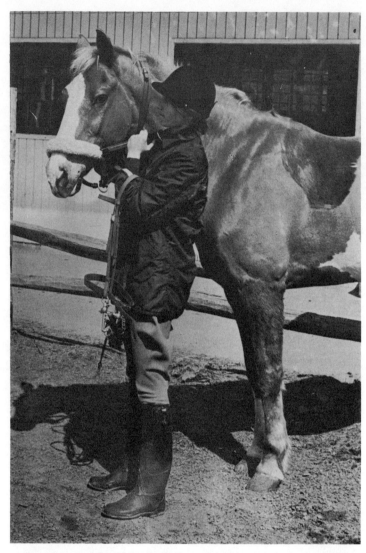

Putting on the halter. If your horse wears a halter, leave the reins behind his ears while you slip it on. This is especially important in a standing stall where he may try to back out.

Carry the saddle over your left arm, the bridle in your right hand. If you want to use your right hand, you can easily hang the bridle on your shoulder, and then you'll have one hand free.

Clean your tack thoroughly each time you ride. Wash the bit first, while it is still damp from the horse's mouth. A quick dip in a pail of water does this. Now hang your

bridle up on a hook and clean every piece of leather. Use saddle soap and a damp sponge. Wrap the sponge around the straps so you clean both sides of the leather and rub the soap in well. If any part is muddy or sweaty, work up a good lather of soap and scrub off the dirt, then rinse off with clean water. Now wring out your sponge as dry as you possibly can, put more soap on it, and rub it into the leather. If, while you are working you want to dampen your sponge without getting it too wet, try dipping your hand in water and rubbing it on the sponge. Don't dip the sponge in unless you want to work up a lather.

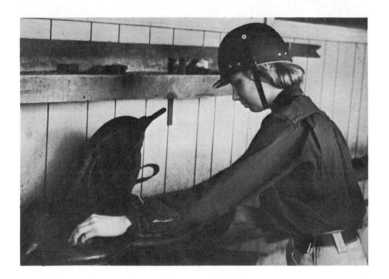

In doing the saddle, turn it upside down and do the lining first. A rack in the form of a trough is very useful for this. If you haven't one, balance the saddle on its throat while you work. When you have done all parts of the saddle run the stirrups up on the leathers again and tuck them into the irons. Be sure to do both sides of the girth. The underside is the most important, for this is the side that touches the horse. Then lay the girth across the saddle and tuck it through the irons.

Here is a saddle beautifully cleaned and all ready to hang up in the tack room.

In hanging up the bridle have it high enough so the reins can hang down their full length.

About once a month take your bridle completely apart. Take the stirrup leathers and the girth guards off the saddle. Now apply a good coat of neatsfoot oil compound to all leather surfaces. Well cared for tack will outlast the horse many times, and a good horseman is known by the condition, and the correct adjustment, of his equipment.

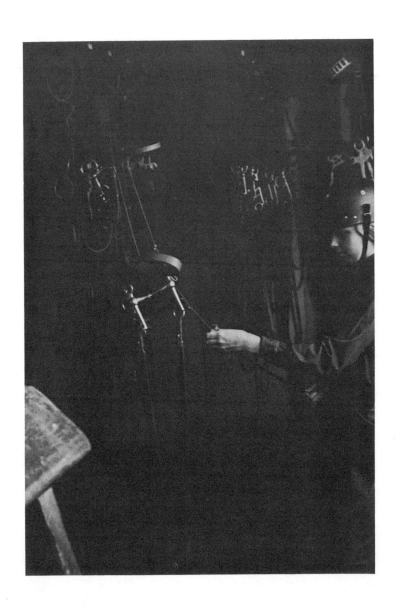

Index

Active hand, 45-46
Adjusting Stirrups, 17-20
Aids, 44-45

Backing, 96-98
Balance position, 28, 69
  at the gallop, 127
Balancing the aids, 59-60
Bight, 11
Bolting, how to cure horse of, 100
Bridle, parts of, 8
Bridling the horse, 147-152
Broken lines, 84

Canter, 118-120
Changing hands, 61, 79-80
Counter canter, 125
Cross canter, 125
Communicating with horse, 43

Diagonals, 74-76
Direct opposition rein, 52
Dismounting, 39-42

Entering the stall, 129-130

Figure 8, 83
Flank movements, 84
Forming pairs at the trot, 94

Gallop, 126-127
Gallop depart, on the diagonal
    aids, 124
  on the lateral aids, 122-123

Grooming, 139

Half turn, 80-82
  in reverse, 82
Halter, 164
Halting, 62-65
Head shy horse, bridling, 150
Horse, points of, 8

Indirect rein of opposition in
    front of withers, 85-86

Jumping around, 115
Jumping off over rump, 116

Leading the horse, 134-138
Leads, 120-121

"Monkey shines," 108-116
  jumping around, 115
  jumping off over rump, 116
  scissors, 108
  standing up on horse, 113
  vaulting on from side, 111
  vaulting over rump, 112
Mounting, 13-17
  preparation for, 10-12
  without a saddle, 104
Musical sacks, 96
Musical stalls, 95-96

Opening, leading rein, 50-51
Opposing the hindquarters with
    the forehand, 14, 15

Passive hand, the, 46-47
Pivot on the hindquarters, 89-90
Pivot around the forehand, 86-88
Position, 27-29
   without a saddle, 104-105
Posting, 68, 71
   practicing, 69-71
   with hands in normal position, 73
   with one hand on waist, 72
Pulley rein, 100

Rearing, curing horse of, 99
Red light, 101
Rein effects, 48-49
   direct opposition, 52
   indirect, 51
   opening, leading, 50-51
Reins, 35-39
   getting right length of, 37
Riding in fours, 94-95
Riding in pairs, 91
  at the trot, 92
  on the right hand, 92-93

Saddle, parts of, 8
Saddling the horse, 155-161
Scissors, 108
Sitting the trot, 67, 79-80
Sitting, 21-26
Standing up on horse, 113
Strong trot, 79-80
Suppling exercises, 29-34
  for arms, 30-31
  for body, 32-33
  for legs, 34
Surcingle, 103

Tack, care of, 166-169
Thrush, 144
Trot, the, 67, 79-80
Turning, 52-57

Vaulting on from side, 111
Vaulting over rump, 112
Volte, 57-58, 79